D0602853

Dad's Pizza

Daniel Levine
Illustrated by Chantal Stewart

My dad loves to make pizza.

"We could open a pizza restaurant!" he says.

DAD'S
ZZA

"We would need lots of flour," Mom says.

DAD'S
ZA
FLOUR
FLOUR
FLOUR
FLOUR

"We would need lots of sauce," Mitzi says.

OIL
OIL
OIL
refrigerate after opening
refrigerate after opening
TOMATO SAUCE
TOMATO SAUCE
TOMATO SAUCE
OLIVES
OLIV

"We would need lots of cheese," I say.

cheese

"We would need lots of toppings," Mom says.

OLIVES
peppers
mushrooms
pepperoni
LIST OF TOPPINGS

"We would need lots of plates," Mitzi says.

Kitchen

"We would need lots of people to wash dishes," I say.

"I think I'll make pizza just for us!" Dad says.
"Let's eat!"